Spinifex

son

This book is about animals that live in the spinifex grass.

CAMBRIDGE
UNIVERSITY PRESS

Spinifex grass grows in the desert.

Australia's deserts are hot, dry places. The sun burns all day, but the nights can be very cold.

Spinifex grass grows in clumps.

Some people call this porcupine grass. Why do you think this is?

A spinifex clump makes a good home for small birds and animals.

Animals hide in the spinifex grass. They find food there. They keep cool by burrowing underneath the spinifex clump.

Small birds build their nests in the spinifex grass.

The Spinifexbird builds its home in the spiky grass. When there is danger, it hides down among the sharp leaves.

The hare-wallaby makes its home in a spinifex clump.

In the daytime the hare-wallaby sleeps in its burrow. Outside, the temperature is over 50 degrees Celsius. Inside, it is cooler, only 30 degrees Celsius.

Spinifex termites use the grass to build their mud castles.

Millions of termites live in this nest. There are soldier termites on guard and blind termites to do the work. The queen lives in a special chamber. It's her job to lay eggs.

Golden Bandicoots live underneath the spinifex.

At night, bandicoots hunt for food. They eat centipedes, termites, moths and sometimes small lizards.

Young bandicoots squabble at night.

The Bilby digs its burrow deep below the spinifex clump.

Water is hard to find in the desert. Most small animals, like the Bilby, get water from the food they eat.

Spinifex Hopping-mice also burrow under the spinifex clump. Their tunnels can be a metre deep.

Hopping-mice have lots of escape holes from their burrows.

Sometimes a snake comes to look for food.

What do the mice do when a hungry snake comes wriggling into their tunnel? They pop up to the surface through an escape hole.

The praying mantis is waiting to pounce on a passing insect.

The praying mantis must keep still among the spines or it could end up as food for a passing bird.

The spider spins a web to catch its food.

This hairy-legged "spider" isn't a spider at all. It's just an empty skin. As a spider grows, its skin gets tight. It can slip out of the old skin and leave it hanging on a spinifex spine.

This little gecko hunts in the spinifex.

The gecko looks for small spiders, grasshoppers and bugs. When it finds some termites or ants, it has a feast.

The Desert Death Adder has found its meal.

The Desert Death Adder hides under spinifex clumps. It feeds on bandicoots or passing lizards. Then, it goes to sleep.

The animals that live in the spinifex grass are safe.

Index